AF480784

THE REOCCURRENCE

OF

LOVE

AND OTHER POEMS

THE

REOCCURRENCE

OF

LOVE

AND OTHER POEMS

STEWART GORDON ROSENBLUM

atmosphere press

CONTENTS

I

II

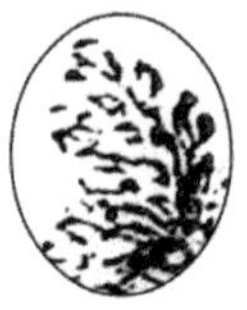

III

IV

V

VI

VII

I

LOVE

AND

THE PERFECT HOUSE

[W]e learned long ago that castles can be drafty.

LOVE

Love finds
what was
in what is,
bestowing youth
upon the aged
and beauty
upon the faded.

It softens
what has hardened
and lives
in eternal hope
that
what never was
will someday be.

A FRIEND

Some may say
that a friend
can not hold
a candle
to a spouse.

But nonetheless,
one may still
achieve the thrill
of sharing
total trust.

And all of this,
without the strain
of trying to maintain
an oft elusive
domestic bliss.

AGE

In youth,
it was far away,
a distant shore
well hidden in time.

En route,
it remained
out of sight,
out of mind.

Now here,
the journey
has proven
far too short.

Just as well
to have retained
some ignorance
along the way.

THE NEWS

The news
doesn't get
better or worse.

It just stays
the same,
each day repeating
the one before.

The headlines
do change,
but the stories
remain the same.

Why can we not fix
this monotonous
record that broke
so long ago?

THE LIE OF THE MIRROR

On her birthday
I told my Cousin
that seventy
is the new fifty.

She agreed, but
was quick to add
that the mirror
often lies.

To be sure, when we look
we do not always see
what is there or
what we need to find.

Rarely will it reveal
a senior's inner child
or the hidden strength trapped
deep inside a timid youth.

And do we not ignore
all that unwanted change
when we put on and then take off
what my late Aunt called the face?

Yet, a mere glance in it
can help us to achieve
whatever we may think
that we want to be.

But for this, why dwell
on a picture so incomplete
that shows us only
what we seek?

Even if a mirror reflects
precisely what it sees,
discerning truth from it
may be hard, indeed.

LOVE 2

Love hopes
that
what never was
will someday be.

The times
when we find love
are also when we feel
most alive.
And conversely,
when love is lost,
we feel quite dead inside.

But we know as well
that what has been lost
may yet be found again.
However, as before,
there is no guarantee
that the love one feels
will be felt by another.

THE PATH

The path that led me here
is littered with zigs and zags,
conceptions and exceptions,
as well as a few
surmises and surprises.

Now that I have lived awhile
and seen a thing or two,
I can be quite certain
that I am always right,
except when I am wrong.

And, with the greatest conviction,
I can proclaim
that the universal truths
are always true,
except when they are not.

It was not always so.
There was a time
when all was new and equally true
and each discovery put a piece
of life's puzzle in its place.

But there were also zigs and zags.
"Because I said so" first arrived
and, if that alone did not suffice,
"Do as I say, not as I do"
became the retort of last resort.

Then, the exceptions came into play.
Sometimes we should and sometimes not.
And, to keep indiscretion at bay,
we learned how and when to rely
on telling a little white lie.

Once confusion had cleared,
absolute certainty appeared.
Independence was then declared and
all the subjects of the realm were held
to a standard achievable by none.

Next came the decades
of running into reality
over and over again,
when we said exactly what we thought
despite what we had been taught.

Explaining this to others
may keep us young at heart,
but when that job is largely done,
the goal before us then becomes
to retire from the fray.

At this time, I do not fear
the uncertainties that persist.
Rather, what remain quite irksome
to this day are the exceptions
that have not lost their bite.

Making peace with them
should preserve the tranquility
we erect against the fragility
that can well result
from having lived awhile.

Better that, than petitioning
for a license to say
precisely what I may,
in a not so quiet voice,
since we all know
how that one ends.

THE RECIPE

To help ensure success
and the desired pliability,
start with two heaping cups
filled with vulnerability.

Each must quickly
touch the other,
or they could well
locate another.

Sharing is essential
to the outcome that you need
and it must take place
in order to proceed.

To speed the union, throw in
a pinch or so of passion and spice,
depending on what you find,
but that alone will not suffice.

Add a mutuality of interests,
much admiration and respect.
Allow to stand and then mix well
in order to achieve what you expect.

Do not allow to boil over.
Rather, let simmer and taste,
lest you find that you end up
with a true mess in your haste.

Once trust has been obtained,
be sure that you have not overdone.
Blend in music, embrace and feel the glow
as two souls begin to dance as one.

Savor, stir and
maintain the heat.
Et voilà, what you now have
should be quite a treat.

A HOME FOR LOST UMBRELLAS

The guest to my right departed
before the dessert had arrived,
leaving his umbrella behind
in a rush to catch the 10:09 train.

When it rains, aren't we grateful
to have an umbrella in hand,
but once it clears, don't we quickly
forget how we came to stay dry?

Cabs, cafes, hotels and the like
must all have outstanding collections
of umbrellas in a vast array
of colors, shapes, prices and sizes.

I gave this no thought until she turned
with eyes twinkling and said
that we need a home for lost umbrellas.
A lost and found was not what she meant.

There, the umbrellas often lie around
in cubicles looking somewhat forlorn,
wondering if anyone sought to inquire
whether they have somehow been found.

No, a home for lost umbrellas would need
to be far more elegant than that,
with a cheery hearth where an umbrella
could dry off from the rain and snow.

And it would certainly have a fully
trained staff whose nurses and doctors
would tie up the loose threads
and mend the occasional tear.

At meals, many choices would have
to be offered, with only fresh food
allowed in this house. But, even so,
would the room be noisy or hushed?

Then came more questions, one after
the other. Who should pay for such care?
Could friends come for a visit?
What if they wanted to stay for tea?

And what might they do all day?
Of course, the library would be stocked
with popular books and the card room
would be full all day and all night.

I can see them being lined up in rows,
repeatedly marching about,
furling and unfurling on cue
to keep both limber and fit.

But what would the neighbors say if such
a refuge were placed in their midst?
Funding would soon be required,
with hordes of advisers very well paid.

As that's enough to make a head spin,
it was well to locate the owner and share
in the relief when the guest to my right
and his lost umbrella were again reunited.

MONEY

Money doesn't care
to whom it belongs,
as my Father would say.

Whether this is just or not
is sometimes hard to know
and beside the point, as well.

Either way, it will not show
much loyalty to station,
family, tribe or nation.

Money will come and go
without uttering either
a goodbye or hello.

And since it rarely lasts,
long term plans for it may be
more illusory than real.

Yet, money will seek out
those who have it, while
bypassing those in need.

Because it does not judge,
it gives scant weight to merit
in choosing a new host.

Some maintain that money is hot.
Although it can burn a hole
in a pocket, it is not.

Rather, it is cold as ice
and will leave one high and dry
without so much as thinking twice.

Having it has never been
a guarantee of taste.
What a genuine waste!

Money takes no notice
of envy and desire,
or even gratitude.

But, once disdained
or spent too freely,
it will disappear.

Inattention, too,
may lead to a separation
that could end up in divorce.

In any case, it doesn't matter
to money who gets to take it home.
After all, it might not be for very long.

LOVE 3

Love finds
what was
in what
is.

At heart,
this is
a largely
selfless act,
conferred
without a thought
of recompense.

But one
that can
help us
to accept
the fearsome toll
that time inflicts
on those we love.

So, too,
it may
provide us
with a way
to forgive
what age has done
to us, as well.

We can
then face
the day
and all it brings
without
the burden
of regret.

So armed
with this
insight,
we may
then seek
what fills us
with delight.

THE PERFECT HOUSE

The perfect house
does not exist
or, if it ever did,
it did not stay that way.

Blame the architect,
fault the engineer,
and don't forget
the zoning board.

As a start,
they placed the house
too near the street
with all its traffic and noise.

But once it snowed,
it somehow seemed
that the house
was too far from the road.

The yard was smaller than needed
until it had to be weeded.
Then, it became a vast expanse,
requiring a crew to maintain.

When full, the house
felt quite cramped,
but over time,
it grew too large.

Even when a house is built
as solid as a rock,
in time it will grow tired
and be in need of paint.

By contrast, structures
that are brand new,
appear to be made
of paper and glue.

As to rooms, there are
either too many or too few.
But while they were at it,
why didn't they add a foot or two?

They should have known
that the piano, alone,
would never fit into
such limited space.

And, after all this time,
why must some quarters
be excessively hot,
while others feel so cold?

What's more, how could
they think that a closet,
so shallow and small,
would be useful at all?

At any rate, the windows
are often in the wrong place
and there is rarely
enough wall space.

Yet, once we accept such flaws
and turn an imperfect house
into our very own home,
we do not want to roam.

Rather, we seek to rest
where we have made our nest.
Besides, we learned long ago
that castles can be drafty.

II

LOVE

AND

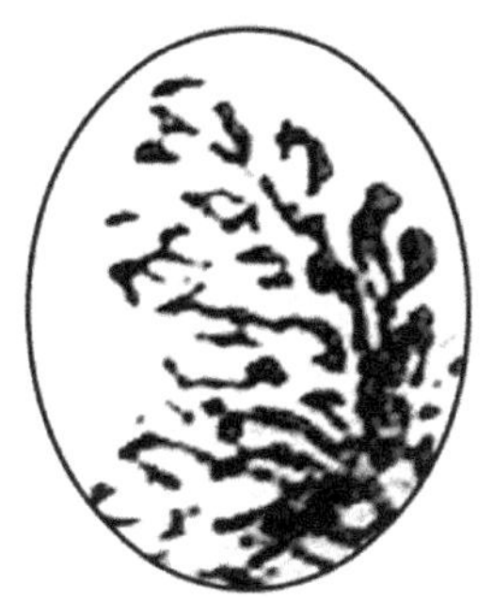

THE SCARSDALE PEACH

Scarsdale is not known for its peaches…

INSIDE AND OUT

The inside and the outside
may be two distinctly
different things.

This should come as no surprise
since few of us believe
we present the way we feel.

It may, however, be
that, at the start,
they began as one.

At any rate, the inner self
and the outer guise will go
their separate ways.

In time, the distance
between them may grow
to be quite great.

Yet, whether young or old,
we do not want the world
to judge us by our shell.

Even when we may seem
to show a lack of warmth,
our core may not be cold.

And, in the course of years,
experience has shown
that appearances deceive.

Calm exteriors
can belie insides
in full panic mode.

Still others take great care
not to reveal a thing
that lies beneath their skin.

Yet, for most of us,
the overriding goal
is to be understood.

Thus, it may be a relief
if, at the end, in and out
are once again in sync.

LOVE 4

Love softens
what has hardened,
and once revealed,
it may induce
the same response
from others.

It sows
the seeds
of compromise
and can forestall
the point
of no return.

Love helps to thaw
what is about
to freeze and adds
some give,
where there is
only take.

It can provide
safe passage
from the storm,
as well as
nourishment
and hope.

Love will melt
a scowl
in a flash
and can bring
a smile
to the face.

And with properties
such as these,
one would think
that we might
value it
far more.

SIR

It was at a homecoming,
under the welcome tent,
that we boys began to reminisce.

More from my brother's class
than from my own appeared,
since it was their forty-fifth.

Being three years younger,
they may have always thought
that I was elderly.

In any case, they claimed
I looked just the same,
despite my white mustache.

With them, I found it hard
to reconcile their gray hair
with the boys they used to be.

Only when they laughed and smiled,
did hints of fifteen peak through
what had become sixty-three.

In the course of conversation,
one spoke of his elation
when someone first called him "sir."

Years and years disappeared
as each of us returned
to our own momentous day.

While the words still echo
in my head, the details
no longer remain clear.

It may well have been
a checkout clerk
who first applied that term.

Of course, I turned around
to see if a man stood
behind me on the line.

Since none was there,
on that day I joined
a most exclusive club.

A club composed of boys
upon whom knighthood
had thereby been conferred.

I must have set off for home
with a smile upon my face,
but somewhat mystified.

An impartial observer
chosen from the world at large
had certified my manhood.

But, how could the world have known
of all the changes that had led
to such a transformation?

LOVE 5

Love
lives
in
eternal hope.

Some seem
to have
an inexhaustible
supply,
but, for most,
encouragement
will help.

Freely given
and received,
the lucky few
find that they
are repaid,
with interest,
and in kind.

In the quest,
it remains
hard to say
how and why
we are drawn
to one and
not another.

Much, of course,
is in the eyes
that behold.
After that,
perhaps we choose
what we like
about ourselves.

Quite often,
this may be
precisely
what we need
to feel
comfortable
and whole.

While the familiar
has real appeal,
there is also
great attraction
to the flames
stoked by what
is not the same.

How complex,
indeed, must
the formula be
to produce
the chemistry
that we seem
to seek.

THE ONION

The layers are
many and deep.
They vary
in thickness
and not all
are sweet.

Outside,
lies the skin,
well shriveled
from time
and the ways
of the world.

Next comes
the public
persona, quite
vibrant and fresh,
but, perhaps,
a bit green.

How one appears
may depend
on who is
observing
and if they like
what they see.

All that
could keep
a publicist
busy, much less
a spokesperson
or two.

How much
to peel back
is always
the question.
Often, just one
layer will do.

The goal is
to locate
a sincere layer
and then
place it
on view.

But, digging deeper
may expose
some selfish,
self-righteous,
judgmental
beliefs.

You know,
the ones
properly
smothered
and mostly
suppressed.

All that suggests,
there is
still more
to explore
before we get
to the core.

LOVE 6

From amongst
the ordinary,
love will locate
what is
extraordinary.

By focusing
upon the good,
it can overlook
what it prefers
not to see.

To bloom,
it only needs
an open door
to find
a kindred soul.

Once aroused,
love will not be
easily suppressed,
despite the odds
against success.

A single
disappointment
will rarely
induce the sick
to seek a cure.

What it takes
is the failure
to attain,
and then retain,
a common ground.

Yet, a mere
reminder
of what was felt
may restore
a ray of hope.

Love will then
pin its hopes
on a dream
that ignores
reality.

In this case,
the act of giving
could turn out to be
the sole reward
that love receives.

By contrast,
the lucky few
are repaid
with interest
and in kind.

MISS ME

Miss me.
I want
to be missed
when I am
gone.

I desire
that someone
care
when I am
not there.

It matters not,
if tears
are shed
when I am
dead.

But, I do wish
to leave behind
a sense of regret
and have others fret
when I am no more.

In point of fact,
there are only
a precious few
who will remember me
just because I was.

My Mother, Father,
Grandparents and maybe
another relative or two
may say that I only
needed to be born.

There may be others
who saw something
to love and recall
in the special times
we have shared.

I do not think
the young comprehend
that just being known
can not begin
to fill the bill.

What is the point
of being linked
forevermore
with the pain
one has caused?

When all is said
and done, I want
others to regret,
not cheer, that
my presence is absent.

Yes, in the end,
like everyone else,
what I want
is to be missed
when I depart.

And, you might think
to tell me so
while I am still here,
for, if you tarry,
it may be too late.

I would like to know
in the hereinbefore,
rather than waiting
until I arrive
in the hereinafter.

THE SCARSDALE PEACH

Insofar as I have heard,
Scarsdale is not known
for its peaches,
precious though they be.

Once my Uncle settled there,
in family circles he became
the Squire of Scarsdale,
for reasons unknown to me.

Perhaps it was the tweed cap,
leather jacket and the Mercedes.
Surely, six tenths of an acre
did not earn him such a title.

No one is left to ask, alas.
However, I am sure
that it did not stem
from cultivating a tree.

The story goes that my Uncle
planted it from a lone peach pit
just behind the house to capture
the light on its southern side.

As the past seems both
rosy and quaint, I picture
my Uncle harvesting
loads of peaches with ease.

There would have been
so many that my Aunt
would have canned them
for friends and family.

In point of fact, I never
saw them take one off the tree
and do not recall talk
of such a large harvest.

Nor do I remember the size
of the crop in my early days
as Lord of the Manor or where
those peaches might have gone.

I do know that it has become
a source of great frustration,
now that I pay attention to
the produce from my estate.

Since I also track the game
found on the grounds, I can say
that, along with deer and rabbits,
squirrels and chipmunks do abound.

I have never seen a rabbit
climb a tree. But the squirrels,
and in some years, the chipmunks,
too, have proven quite adept.

It does not matter how big
or ripe the fruit. Whether it
sits on the tree or the ground,
they believe it's theirs to take.

They show no hesitation
to remove every last one
and leave me with a harvest
that consists of none.

I am convinced my sole recourse
is to dine out on tales of woe,
since I would starve if I had
to depend on what they leave for me.

When I go to market
and see a perfect peach,
I can only marvel
at the grower's success.

I once asked a Jersey farmer
about pests who steal his fruit.
He said none came near the trees
in the orchards that he owns.

I guess that he does not back up
to a woods and has no oak trees
in his front yard. Yet, it seems odd
that they have missed such a treat.

I don't know what I can do
to expand my take next year,
unless I get a subsidy
or get paid not to grow fruit.

Frankly, I would rather have
a bushel of mouthwatering
peaches grown in Scarsdale
on which I could feast.

THE TRANSFORMATION OF MAGIC

To begin with
there was wonder
in the magic
of it all.

What satisfaction
we felt when we made
that square peg fit
into the square hole.

And with a mere blanket,
we could make things
disappear and then
reappear upon command.

Yet, over time, the wonder
vanished, along with the magic,
doomed by familiarity and
the basic laws of physics.

Even the sleight of hand
became a trick to be
practiced and admired, but
no longer wondrous, in itself.

Yet, all has not been lost,
although the wonder of magic
may no longer be the element
that continues to enthrall.

Rather, what now seems
to excite the soul
and quicken the pulse
is the magic of wonder.

The wonder is found
throughout the universe.
The magic of its creation
and operation still astound.

Even great minds struggle
to grasp something so immense
and intricate. The more we learn,
the greater the wonder grows.

We humans seem quite able
to make nothing out of something,
destroying what is in our way
or that we can not comprehend.

Yet, creating something physical
out of nothing eludes us
to this day, so perhaps that
is still best left to the divine.

THE YOUNG

The young
are armed
with naiveté,
elasticity
and hope.

As youth
begins
to fade away,
naiveté may
take its leave as well.

In its place,
experience
can supply
the arms and armor
needed for the fight.

Certainty,
shrewdness and
wisdom will, no doubt,
be called up
to the front.

Hope can provide
the inspiration
and elasticity
may soothe
the wounds incurred.

As elasticity
decreases over time,
dressing for battle
may become
a real ordeal.

If hope
is also lost,
experience,
alone, will
act as guide.

It can attest
to the value
of somehow
remaining
young at heart.

And, it may show
how to regain
the elasticity,
naiveté and hope
that sadly have been lost.

Perhaps,
the key may be
never to surrender
one's wonder
at it all.

THEN AGAIN

Oh!
What a pain
it is to die
and, one by one,
to give up
everyone
and everything
that you ever
loved,
as well as
every dream
and hope
that you ever
had.

THEN AGAIN,
I can feel
the burden
lifting now.
What a huge relief
to be free
of every
missed opportunity
and failed attempt,
along with
each bitter memory
and lingering regret
that could have weighed
me down.

It might well be
that's it. Finito!
So sorry my dears.
The world will have
to get along
without the likes
of me. Too bad,
for, as with most,
I have left so much
undone.
Perhaps another
will simply take
my place
in line.

THEN AGAIN,
that other may share
my DNA,
or, if not,
at least hold dear
my firmly held beliefs
and acquired tastes,
along with those hopes
and dreams
that made me
who I was,
or, at least,
whom I thought
I wished to be.

THEN AGAIN,
what a thrill
it would be,
to come back
and start over
with a clean slate.
Or, better yet,
perhaps
I could return
with some knowledge
as my guide
in order to avoid
the mistakes I made
the last time around.

Regardless of what
the hereafter may bring,
I am certain that
somewhere, sometime,
somehow the sun
will warm a cheek
and a delicious breeze
will stir a soul.
And who am I,
pray tell,
that I should
be so bold
as to ask
for more
than that?

REMEMBRANCES

I keep them all
close at hand,
my Mother
in the refrigerator
and my Father
in the drawer.

And then, there is
the Grandmother
who sits by the window
while the other
is ever ready
to see the light of day.

Each has a mate
not far away.
One Grandfather
is on the hutch
and the other awaits
reuse nearby.

That is to say,
I keep cool and
safe an unopened
Mason jar of jam
that my Mom made
long before she died.

And in the drawer
is the silver plated
soup spoon from a set
my Dad recalled
from his youth
so long ago.

By the window
in an age-old pot
is a plant
that my Grandmother
had tended almost
fifty years before.

A rack from a steamer
used by the Grandmother
whom I never met
seems to add
a special something
to the turkey I prepare.

And in the dining room
sits the soup tureen
that the Grandfather
who died before my time
brought home one day.
We don't know when or why.

The library desk
now holds
the magnifying glass
all splattered with
my Grandfather's
paint by numbers oils.

But for this poem,
who else would know
when I am gone
where to find
these treasures
I have saved?

LOVE 7

Love finds
what was
in what is.
With contact,
it can bridge
the now
and the then
by filling in
what has been lost.

And whether or not
familiarity
has bred
contempt,
a sense
of security
may also permit
the love
to be sustained.

But once
a separation
in time and space
has fully dimmed
the spark
that had entranced,
what is left
to captivate
the heart?

The memory
of what excited
and once delighted
may survive
and briefly ignite
the old flame.
Yet it may lack
enough power
to restart the fire.

How odd it is
after much passion
to retain
only the memory
of a love
and to recall it
without feeling heat
by looking on
as a mere voyeur.

Even when
encountering
the former object
of desire,
it could well be
that any stirring
will only be noted
from a clinical
point of view.

HOW MUCH IS ENOUGH?

How old
do you have
to be
to know
better?

How long
do you have
to wait
to learn when
to move on?

How smart
do you have
to be
to see the truth
before your eyes?

How lucky
do you have
to be
to appreciate
how lucky you are?

How grateful
do you have
to be
to express
your gratitude?

How wrong
do you have
to be
to make
it right?

If not yet,
what will
it take
to make
it now?

A LIFE

As a life
it was
the same
as others,
that is to say,
quite distinct.

Since nothing
out of the
ordinary
occurred,
it was unique,
like all the rest.

Unmatched
either before
or since,
it was special
in its
own right.

Endlessly repeated,
it proved
to be a
tour de force
that would not
be seen again.

Each joy
and sorrow
was perceived
by it
in a way
no other would.

In this way
a point of view
emerged,
drawn from
what life
had taught.

Over time,
both its novelty
and its
commonality
became fully
evident.

In the end,
it proved to be
remarkable,
a life
much like
any other.

THE COUNTDOWN

The countdown
to extinction
has begun.
Actually,
it commenced
when life began.

If we continue
to learn and
stay active,
we may succeed
in ignoring
the clock.

A variety
of interests
and obligations
can ensure that one
is suitably
occupied.

And then,
there are
the emergencies
that one
must face
and overcome.

Not to mention,
a job or two
and the needs
of others
who depend
on you.

In the end,
there may
not be
a lot of time
to dwell
on mortality.

Since
we cannot
change it,
devoting
much thought to it
just wastes
our precious days.

Yet,
it remains
hard to forget
that a clock
is ticking
softly
at our back.

III

LOVE

AND

A COUNTRY GARDEN

A rabbit spied the beets…

THAT WORLD IS GONE

That world is gone.
Precious little of it
survives to this day.
Scattered bits, faded portraits
and traits in descendants
are all that remain.

Someone brought an oval
cooking pot with handles
and a foreign mark,
made of copper lined with tin.
It was saved, but in my time,
it only held houseplants.

On one side, eight siblings came.
Older brothers were the first.
Starting in iron, they might
have merged with Bethlehem Steel.
In the end, it was fortunate
that they wound up in real estate.

So, Sam became
a developer and
a party leader in Queens.
He had a way with people.
"Professor," as he was called,
had a pince-nez and mustache.

Sadie, his bride and
mother of his son
and six daughters,
is seen adoring him
in their wedding
photograph.

In the later photos,
the ones in gilded frames,
he looks quite distinguished,
but the spark in her seems gone.
That is what illness can do,
when it lasts for years.

I know almost nothing
of his parents or of hers
whom my Mother said were
quite sweet. Just as well,
since Sam put them in business
operating a candy shop.

Along with the copper pot,
a cellaret, two benches,
a bedroom set and chair,
there are books, china,
and candlesticks to help
recall that they were here.

Each tells us something
of their wants and dreams.
Grandpa was said to read
the adventures in wonderland
each year, but did he open
his volumes of Locke and Hume?

And did he know that
the Royal House of Hanover
ordered a set of china
from the same company
that made the tureens
he brought home one day?

With his nickname and mustache
and her revealing eyes,
I try to imagine
what life was like
in their household
one hundred years ago.

Endless summers at the beach
before the hurricane,
entertaining relatives each week,
as well as politicians,
judges and the police.
It surely was another world.

I should have asked
my Mother more questions
and taken careful notes,
since now I have forgotten
some things that may be
important to relate.

I do know who I am,
after a considerable
amount of time,
but it would have been
helpful to know more
about how and why.

COLLECTING

At heart,
many of us
are collectors.
It could well be
in our very bones.

Sometimes, the chase
for the must haves
becomes a sport,
one followed closely
by its avid fans.

After all,
you never know
when you may need
one or more
of these or those.

Curiosity
may spur us on.
We found one,
but wonder what else
there could be.

Perhaps we need
to complete
the series
and fill in
every gap.

Arranging them
in order
and putting all
in their place
may also reassure.

Oh, the joy
of comparing
this and that,
while noting
how they differ.

We value some
for their beauty,
while others
are greatly prized
for their rarity.

Sometimes,
it is hard
to judge
what will stand
the test of time.

Surely, one's taste
can change
and the favored
may no longer
be admired.

What was rare
may become
mass produced
and its charm
may disappear.

And, in the end,
some ideas
may prove great
only when shared
for the first time.

Others may enthrall
for years
and provide
a welcome respite
from one's cares.

Such attributes
are shared
by collections
of both things
and people.

Things do possess
some advantages.
They listen well
and are quite
dependable.

Their beauty may be
slow to fade
and they return
all the regard
they receive.

With people,
far less is certain.
One should not expect
there to be
a guarantee.

Yet, unlike things,
people have
the capacity
to give back more
than they receive.

Apparently,
with more risk
comes the potential
of a greater
reward.

THAT GREEN

That special green
is miraculous
each and every year,
a combination
of science
and expectation,
like much of what we see.

Not confined
to a single hue,
we are treated
to a pale light green,
a vivid yellow green,
as well as all
that lies between.

It could be the light,
the intensity and
the angle of its rays,
or the way in which
the early morning dew
affects what comes
within our gaze.

Perhaps it is
biochemistry
at work
and that green
can just not keep pace
with its expanding
universe.

Thin layers
and rapid growth
may well produce
the translucent,
just washed look
that we note
in early Spring.

What makes it special
could be the contrast
with what came before
when green was absent,
or that for a time,
the transition
remains incomplete.

We may recognize,
as well, the green
that we have used
to celebrate
rebirth
and renewal
since time began.

In any case,
Spring green differs
from that of Summer
when green is strong,
self-assured
and clearly
in its prime.

Nor is it like Fall,
when heat and drought
have worn down
green's confidence
and hints of age appear,
foretelling
what will come.

No, there is truly
something special
about the green
of Spring
and the innocence
and purity
it projects.

Those tender,
determined buds
and vibrant,
refreshed spikes
in which we so rejoice
offer us the hope
of a fresh start.

The floral display
in yellow and white
as green reclaims
the field
may also enhance
the freshness that we feel
at this time of year.

Overnight
it seems,
pale shoots arise
to assess the climate.
The bravest of them
set off an explosion
of new green leaves.

Having emerged naively
from their tight wrappers,
the leaves of Spring
have yet to suffer
the indignity
of being blown about
and eaten by insects.

That will soon give way
to Summer's sturdier,
thicker green canvass,
marking the passage
to the next season
and the onslaught
that awaits.

THE GLOW OF AGE

"They" say,
as my Mother would say,
that people
become happier
as they age.
Whoever the they
may have been,
what they said
could well
have been true.

The other day
I did feel it.
I was just standing there,
minding my own business
and then it happened.
Induced by body chemistry,
a naturally occurring glow
began on its own,
spreading happiness
throughout my frame.

Since I do not know
its formula, I can not
produce huge quantities
and begin any kind
of marketing campaign.
Besides, I think
it is far better
to have lived awhile
and to manufacture
one's own supply.

THE PERSISTENCE OF PRIVILEGE

Privilege has again
reared its ugly head,
causing me to ask
what has brought it back.

I am sure that it begins
when we pay no mind.
And, once it starts,
it grows quite rapidly.

It spreads as well,
but not too far. After all,
what would the appeal be,
if everyone enjoyed some?

The problem often comes
when the populace is asleep.
People may not recognize
what is in their midst.

If there is no regard
for history and the lessons
that it can teach, privilege
may gain the upper hand.

With it, come prerogatives,
such as power, authority,
and entitlement, all based
on certainty of merit.

These are the things
that make it hard
to overthrow unless pressure
is successfully applied.

And once privilege
feels at home
and takes root,
it will tend to last.

So, once it appears,
privilege may well stay,
given how hard it is
to drive away.

ALONG THE WAY

You know full well
that you are getting old
when certain things occur,
but here I do not refer
to the white hair
and wrinkles
kind of age.

Rather, it is
when you are sure
that you have already seen
the latest fashions,
but this time,
unlike the last,
they look ridiculous.

What was regarded
as noise in your youth
would be judged
to be quite melodic,
at least compared
to some of what passes
as music today.

The derisive
adjectives
once applied
to the Masters
of the past
seem appropriate
for describing some art
that is currently hot.

The foods
that were regarded
as quite unhealthy
have now been found
to be a useful
part of your diet
and beneficial
to your health.

Notwithstanding
all of the above,
I am optimistic
that this, too, shall change
and I remain convinced
that the generation
coming to the fore
is not beyond hope.

So, in short,
while I am clearly
not as young
as I used to be,
it is also true
that I am
not as old
as I wish to be.

COMPROMISE

We learn to compromise
before we walk or talk.
When crying does not
get us what we want,
unless distracted,
we must come
to accept our lot.

Yet, with debating skills
supplemented by pleading,
wheedling and
a tantrum or two,
we are able to educate
our elders in the art
of compromise.

In fact,
living
in a family
might be seen
to be an endless
opportunity
to practice compromise.

Learning to balance
dreams and
aspirations
with an acceptance
of limitations
can be difficult,
indeed.

Compromising
our hopes
for those
we hold dear
may be
especially hard
to bear.

The same
is true
of decisions
in careers,
as well as
those we make
while life unfolds.

How many can say
no compromises
were made
when choosing
a partner, profession,
home, colleague
or friend?

So what makes
politicians think
that applying the art
of compromise
that they learned at home
has no place
in a public forum?

SHE SAID

She said
that she said
that after a while
husbands are just
excess baggage.

What an intriguing
statement! It sounds
so authoritative
and definitive
that it must be true.

Or, is it like
so much else today
that bears little resemblance
to the truth once it has been
examined carefully.

Perhaps it is true
in one case or another.
Yet, that hardly
makes it
the norm.

But, what does
it really mean
and when should
we expect
that it would apply?

Is this a question
of gender? What if
the claim were made
that wives became
excess baggage?

Perhaps it reflects
the failure of romance
to grow into friendship
with the passage
of time.

Or, is it a cry
of the self
yearning to be free
after all is said
and done?

With this in mind
I am left to wonder
how the original
job description
was worded.

A COUNTRY GARDEN

First,
I planted beets,
so I could make
a pot
of borscht.

A rabbit
spied the beets
and thought
they were
for him, alone.

So then,
I planted
radishes
and achieved
the same result.

I decided
not to buy
a gun
and try to end
the rabbit's life.

Instead,
I chose
to add
onions
to the plot.

Seeing
such a
fancy feast,
the rabbit
invited friends.

They were
most kind
and left
some onions
in the ground.

The problem is
that onions
really
don't agree
with me.

So now,
I have
a question
that remains
to be resolved.

How many onions
does it take
to buy
a pot
of borscht?

ALONG FOX MEADOW

They stand quite bare
and gaunt in March,
those relics
of a bygone
past.

With massive feet
planted firmly
in the ground,
they seem to have been
around forever.

In two rows
along the sides
of the road,
they line up
almost trunk to tail.

As I pass them by,
they appear to process
down the street
at a glacial
pace.

Heavy and
ponderous,
they tower
above all
in their midst.

But, ravaged
by time,
there are gaps
where others
once stood.

No trace
remains
as to how
those relatives
met their end.

Though often
bent over
and missing limbs,
the survivors seem
too large to fall.

Deeply furrowed,
their bodies
tilt toward
the light and food,
defying gravity.

Stumps projecting
in mid-air
like sawed-off tusks,
tell of the injuries
they have endured.

How different
it must have been
when they were young
and among the first
to frequent the lane.

Long before
their wrinkles and
the Dutch disease,
they were spritely
and straight.

Now, birds of prey
perched on high
survey the landscape,
hoping to feed
on what scurries below.

Once clothed in leaves,
the elms of Fox Meadow
may yet again shed
their elephantine
appearance.

THE LITTLE VOICE

There is
a little voice
inside of me
that has
been there
for a while.

It speaks softly
just before
I opine
in a way
I will soon
regret.

Others
have one, too,
but also fail
at times
to mind
its sage advice.

As they choose
their words,
I have seen
a smile
spread
across their face.

After that
eureka moment,
out will pour
something that
they should not
say.

Once the words
have been spoken,
it becomes
too late
to take
them back.

If only
we could slow
things down
for just
a fraction
of a second.

Maybe, then,
the little voice
would have
a chance
to be heard
a second time.

Silently
repeating
what Ramona
was told
might well
do the trick.

"You don't
have to have
an opinion
about everything,"
her spouse
would state.

Such advice
might help us heed
the little voice
when it warns us
not to say
what we think.

EXPECTATIONS

If you count yourself
among those
whose expectations
have not been
fulfilled,
you are hardly
alone.

How many
can truly say
they have achieved
what they set out
to do?
I am sure
it's only a few.

The reasons
for this
are many
and often not
of our choosing.
Among others, there is
the element of chance.

And, there are those
born or raised
without hope
or expectations.
They must begin
by creating
some of each.

For the ones
who do make their way,
it can be
a thrilling ride.
But, the odds
of success
are not always great.

More realistic,
perhaps,
is to accept
that more likely
than not,
we could well
come up short.

A bit
of age
or an old soul
might allow us
to limit
how much
we regret.

How useful, then,
to come to grips
with compromise
and add that wisdom
to enthusiasm
when passing the dream
along.

LIMITS

We all have
our limits
that determine
just how far
we will go.

When based
on principle,
not prejudice,
they need not
be shed.

The ones
of our making
are where
the dangers
lie.

We know
they often
represent
a failure
to grow.

But, how far
should we strain
against
our own
instincts?

And where
shall we look
to replace
the comforts
that limits provide?

Maybe
the way
to proceed
is to take
small steps.

We may find that
not all habits
are essential.
Some may well be
detrimental.

How foolish, then,
not to explore
a bit outside
the lines
that we have drawn.

IV

LOVE

AND

GOING OUT AND ABOUT

[A] whole world exists
out there…

PERFECTION

I am convinced
that each of us
attains the peak
of perfection
at a given
time in life.

To be clear,
I do not mean
the pinnacle
of our strength
or mental
acuity.

Rather,
I refer
to how
we rate ourselves
compared to those
we regard as peers.

We all know
some mature early
and reach their peak
in high school
as the king
and queen of prom.

Others wait
until college
to sprout
and then become
the most
admired.

Through all that
and more,
I have waited
patiently
for my time
to arrive.

My peak
has indeed
been slow
in coming,
but its day
may soon appear.

How exciting
to have a cause
for celebration
after the passage
of so many
years.

Nonetheless,
I am not sure
that I prefer
to look back on it
as something
in my past.

Yet, if my peak
waits too long,
it may find
that the window
of opportunity
has already closed.

THE ORDER

The package
that arrived
was not
what was
expected.

Good thing
we knew
the results
were not
guaranteed.

All parts
were received,
but it seemed
much was left
to chance.

Nonetheless,
it was clearly
the order
we had
placed.

Fortunately,
we did not need
an exact
mini-us,
after all.

While not precisely
what we wished for,
our goal became
to make the best
of what we got.

Besides, the package
did not contain
a postage paid
return address
label.

TOO LATE, MY LOVE

While love may still
quicken the heart,
repeated hurt
will soon turn
what was unbridled
into something
far more guarded.

This is not
a case of
feigned disdain
or a playful flirt
in what is
an ongoing game
of cat and mouse.

Rather,
how perverse
it is
that sparing
no effort
often produces
no response.

Yet, once hope
has been surrendered,
replaced by distance
and an unspoken chill,
note may be taken
of efforts
long ignored.

Why do we wait
until the horse
has left the barn
to notice
its absence
and then express
regret?

Why do we want
what we can not
have
and refuse
what is often
within
our grasp?

If we could find
a reason
for this
other than
the heart wants
what the heart wants,
we would know it
by now.

AFTER THE STORM

Saturday morning
the sun returned
after the snow had ended,
as if nothing untoward
had occurred.

The dusting
that was predicted
to be washed away
had instead
decided to stay.

Outside the window
I spied
a massive, furry
clump of black
on an old azalea plant.

Too large for a mouse,
or even a dreaded rat,
a young squirrel
was a much better,
more agreeable choice.

Staying so still,
its situation
was unclear,
as squirrels rarely
seem to sleep on the job.

Possibly,
it had never
seen snow before
and did not know
what to do.

Some day we may learn
how a squirrel thinks
and understand
more of what
humans say and do.

For example,
why did bananas
become the sticking point
when offered at the end
of a visit home?

Perhaps, there is
no mystery after all.
Periodically,
a child must show
some independence.

And what better way
to assert
autonomy
than to refuse
bananas.

THE WAY

The longer
that I live,
the farther
that I roam,
the deeper
my understanding
of how others
spend their time,
the more
I am convinced
that the way
I live my life
suits me.

LOVE 8

I am looking,
but I do not see.
I am listening,
but I do not hear.
I am aching,
but I do not feel.

I am searching,
but I can not find
what initially
attracted
me
to you.

So now,
the question is
what,
if anything,
is
to be done.

Should the life
I know
be enough
to keep me near?
And, are there others
I must consider?

After all the years
in tandem,
will I be able
to re-grow the parts
that have
atrophied?

And what
makes me think
that the untried
would likely
outshine
the familiar?

Yet,
will there ever be
a better time
than the present
to take a break
or make a stand?

I doubt that waiting
to be older
or more experienced
will increase
the odds
of success.

But, perhaps,
what has
been lost
may yet
be found
again.

And starting
the conversation
might help
unearth
what first
attracted me.

At least, it might
enable me
to keep alive
the thought
that an attraction
once existed.

THE FEW

How lucky
are the few
who know
what they want
to do.

How happy
are the rare
who have
good fortune
to spare.

How thrilled
are the small quantity
who recognize
when they come across
the best quality.

How blessed
are the limited number
who are visited
by the muse
while they slumber.

How joyous
are the fraction
who have found
that love acts
as their bastion.

How fortunate
are the paucity
who are able
to bounce back
from adversity.

How triumphant
are the pittance
who do succeed
in leaving envy
at a distance.

How privileged
are the minority
who retain
both health and wealth
in seniority.

And how content
are the handful
who possess
the good sense
to be grateful.

GOING OUT AND ABOUT

Sometimes,
as I prepare
to go out,
I wonder
fleetingly
if I shall be
coming back.

I look around
with pleasure
at the home
that is mine,
with all
I have arranged
to suit my fancy.

I think to myself
what a shame
it would be
if I could not
come back
to what I have
created.

As I ponder this,
I recognize
that the odds
of being able
to return
remain heavily
in my favor.

Besides,
a whole world
exists out there
to be explored,
enticing me
to venture forth
yet again.

NO NEED

He(she)knew
that she(he)knew.
And,
he(she)knew
that she(he)knew
that he(she)knew
that she(he)knew.

In view
of all
that knowledge,
they chose
to discuss
other
things.

LOVE 9

```
Love
is determined
to find
what it seeks
whether it is
there or not.

It remains
convinced
that
what it gives
must be
returned.

And, since
enthusiasm
is catching,
love is confident
that it will
be caught.

Yet, despite
such certainty,
love can not believe
its good luck
when it achieves
success.
```

ONGOING

Think of how much time
we spend attempting
to change others
while also seeking
to remake ourselves.

Sometimes isolated,
but often in concert,
we expend this effort
in order to carve out
our place in the world.

Each day we set about
looking to close the gap
between who we are
and who we wish
to be.

And, in this pursuit
we plan, negotiate
and sometimes oppose
the will of others
similarly engaged.

We sometimes forget
this is far easier
when sustenance and shelter
are assured and peace
is at hand.

THE MAKEOVER

There is so much
to change
about those we love
that it is hard
to know
where to begin.

Not only is this
a noble goal,
helping them to grow,
but it might also
be a way to restore
one's sanity, as well.

Polishing the rough edges
and focusing on
the traits that grate
would surely be
a good
start.

The things that never meshed
were once either funny
or could be overlooked.
The fact that they are
so predictable
is what now causes stress.

And, once our beloveds receive
the makeover they deserve,
humanity could be next
as it, too, is
in desperate need
of change.

THE ARTS

In the arts
of all types
there are
creators
of all stripes.

Whatever their description,
when it comes
to explanation,
the makers will rarely
get the last word.

While the artists may
point out the way,
others are always
free to have
their own say.

Sometimes,
the process is
collaborative,
at other times,
combative is more apt.

For once the makers decide
that their endeavors
should be shared,
nothing requires that they
or their work must be spared.

THE FOUNDERS

As time marches on,
the ranks of the founders
start to thin out.

They begin to fade away,
appearing less often
than in the past.

While still determined,
they may act as observers
rather than as creators.

And, so they come
to assume the mantle
of institutional memory.

In the end, one of them
must be the last to go,
perhaps treasured, perhaps less so.

If successful, something
more long lasting than they
will remain to be savored.

It will then be for the stewards
who come next to inspire
the generations that follow.

THE LIMITS OF FAME

From the very beginning
until the end is upon us,
it seems quite clear
that we wish
to be heard.

Those who seek fame
want that, of course,
but may also
be looking for
something more.

Despite efforts to deny,
deflect and dissemble,
isn't the search for fame
an attempt to prolong
a finite existence?

Fame is indeed a way
to have hordes you never met
utter your name
with admiration or dread,
but how effective is that?

After all, what's in a name
when it is divorced
from body and soul,
having been forced to part
from its true owner?

And, over the course of time,
doesn't that disembodied name
take on a life of its own,
separate and apart
from its original bearer?

So, in the end,
if the name has little
or no relation
to the original creation,
what does that accomplish?

How much does that help us
obtain what we crave,
when we frantically seek
what we suspect
we can not have?

V

LOVE

AND

POEMS ARE LIKE CHILDREN

You do what you can and
hope for the best.

LIVING FOR ART

Some believe
that art is important
and that struggle
is a useful
first step.

Struggle may well
heighten the senses,
focus the mind
and keep routine
at bay.

After breaking free,
what a joy it is
to be lost
in thought
while art is created.

Hunger and thirst must wait.
Time may slip by
without notice
and the clock
is not seen or heard.

What a contrast to boredom!

LOVE 10

What has
been lost
may yet
be found
again.

Perhaps,
this is one
of those things
that is easier
said than done.

First, there is
the search
that may take
a fair amount
of time.

How hard
one looks
may well depend
on the extent
of need.

Of course,
it helps
if one knows
what one
seeks.

It may be
companionship,
intimacy,
excitement,
care, love or all
of the above.

So, then,
the equation
is complex,
even before
one thinks
of adding sex.

ODE TO THE GLORY OF YOUTH

How glorious it is
to be young,

to be undaunted,
flexible and eager,

to be questioning,
open and earnest,

not to be discouraged
by failure and fragility,

or disappointed
by time and betrayal,

and best of all,
blessed with certainty,

knowing that a fresh perspective
can cure almost anything,

unencumbered by experience
and the wisdom that may come with age.

LOVE 11

How can it be
that I think
so much of you
and you think
so little of me?

Why is it that
I ask how you are
and what you think,
but you rarely ask
the same of me?

Why is what you do
of interest to me,
whereas nothing
that I enjoy
seems to excite you?

Why do I try
to make time for you,
but your schedule
has no room in it
for me?

Why do I seek
more ways to connect,
while you ignore
the ones
that already exist?

So, in the face
of such obstacles,
what can explain
the motivation
to persist?

Perhaps one reason
is that we are taught
to love ourselves
and to respect
our admirable traits.

So, it is difficult
to understand
how and why others
may be unable
to do the same.

Yet we know
that the situation
is often reversed.
Then, we are the ones
who remain unmoved.

Maybe we all
could do more
to recognize that
the regard of others
is precious.

THE GAP

Reality
may be
a friend
or a foe,
greeting
expectations
with either
joy or woe.

Yet,
failing
to hope
or plan
rarely
provides
a path
to success.

So,
just mind the gap
and watch
your step,
since the future
remains
quite hard
to predict.

WHY?

"Why?" he asked,
over and over again,
each response producing
yet another question
until his Mother
was sure that she could not
endure more.

Thankfully, a stranger
volunteered that it was
a sign of intelligence,
precisely the thing
she needed to hear
in order to survive
the incessant onslaught.

Someone has to bring
order to the universe,
putting all in context
for those just starting out,
explaining the way
the world works
and the nature of things.

That quest for knowledge
by one so young was largely
innocent at heart,
a search for answers
when faced with a barrage
of new experiences
that required explanation.

Repeatedly asking, "Why?"
might also have been
a way to engage
in a game of give and take
that ensured the receipt
of parental attention,
something that all children want.

At a later date, "Why?"
was put to good use
in questioning custom
and authority,
proving how powerful
a single syllable
can be.

THE DANCE

He was too old
to be considered
a toddler,
too big
for the stroller
that his Mother
had brought for him,
on a day far too long
for someone his age
to be anything but
inconsolable by then,
stuck in a train car
that was too old, too hot
and too crowded to be
anything but uncomfortable.

Returning from the shore,
he did not notice
that his Mother winced
each time he shifted his weight
standing on her seated thighs,
but the rest of the car did,
in silent sympathy
with his frustration
and his Mother's plight,
as she wondered
how she could ever
have thought
the day would end
other than
disastrously.

It was the rump
part of a Sunday,
the worst time
of the week for many,
that portion of the day
when the fun of the weekend
was definitely over
and there was nothing more
to look forward to,
when the reality
of the coming work week
becomes apparent and
the only remaining option
is to tackle what had been
neglected all weekend.

Over time, his shifting
became a dance,
until he finally
plaintively informed her
that he needed to pee,
whereupon, they set off
to find a latrine,
undoubtedly returning
before the journey
had ended, but I have
no recollection of that,
as it was apparently
less memorable than
what had preceded
their departure.

WHAT'S THE RUSH?

The older I get,
the less inclined
I am to want
to rush, and thus
the more I try
to plan, so that
I need not hurry.

However, I start
each day with list
in hand and seek
to cross the items
off one by one
before the day
is done.

Tick tock. It must
happen today,
just in case
there may be
no tomorrow,
or so I appear
to think.

And yet, as I am in
retirement mode,
I also believe
that what I can
not do today,
I may leave
for tomorrow.

At present,
the goal
is to enjoy
the equilibrium
between being busy
and being able
to extend deadlines.

That seems to provide
just enough stress
and pressure
such that time
is not wasted,
but not so much
as to fray the nerves.

For the lucky few,
who can still do
and also find
a way to limit
their wear and tear,
this is a course
they might pursue.

THE ARTIST'S TORMENT

There is
great joy
when an artist
with something
to say
is discovered.

Yet, many artists
are haunted
by self-doubt
and fear
they have nothing
much to offer.

After their first
breakthrough,
they often live
in dread
that it could be
their last.

And so they search
for something new
that could produce
their next success
and vault them
to the top.

Once found,
they are sure
it is the answer
to their prayers
and will result
in their best work.

That is, until
they decide
to change course
in order to pursue
their next
great idea.

Along the way,
dealers, critics
and collectors
all have their say
as to what they think
has merit.

Different critiques
tend to come and go,
as if the torment
already endured
had not been more
than adequate.

POEMS ARE LIKE CHILDREN

Poems are
like children,
each a miracle
at birth.

So perfect, precious
and well formed,
they all are special
in their own way.

Many do their work
in short order.
A few require
extra time.

There are those
that appear
forward, while others
seem quite shy.

What you see
is what you get
applies to some,
but not to all.

Poems are
like children.
You do what you can
and hope for the best.

BE FORTUNATE

In the midst
of the pandemic
his recommendation
was simple.
"Be fortunate,"
he said.

Surely that is
good advice,
not only then,
but throughout
the whole
of your life.

Since you cannot
choose your parents,
the best thing
is to be fortunate
as to the ones
that you get.

In the choice
of a mate,
it is beneficial
to be fortunate
in the selection
that you make.

You may not be able
to control who lives
further down the hall
or elsewhere on the block.
Good fortune may be
what is needed.

You are fortunate
if you are in
the right place
at the right time,
and not
somewhere else.

It could be fate,
predestination
or just the luck
of the draw.
Whatever the case,
Be Fortunate.

THE CLOCKS

The family
is awash
in clocks.
Inherited
burdens,
they sometimes
seem.

Now advanced
in years,
they have grown
temperamental
and somewhat
obsolete,
as well.

Invented
long ago,
you would
think
they might
behave more
reliably.

As with plants,
they insist upon
occupying
a comfortable place
before agreeing
to keep good time
or run at all.

What makes
them stop,
I do not know.
Regardless,
time, by contrast,
will not
stand still.

Each requires
a different
number of turns
when being
wound,
not too many,
not too few.

So, tending
to them
has become
a full time job.
What's more,
one always seems
to need repair.

Bearing traits
of former owners
is not that rare.
One clock continues
to run fast,
just like
its late mistress.

Another appears
to be quite
finicky,
even though
it occupies
its accustomed place
on the mantel piece.

Yet, there is
something
reassuring
about hearing
regular
tick tocks and
a chime.

And,
those that run
on atmospheric
pressure, alone,
add a silent
mystery
to a home.

EXCAVATIONS

It does not seem fitting
to reduce a life
to a box or two,
especially,
the life of one
so lively and engaged,
now shrunken
to a few stacks
of strangely random,
hardly representative
odds and ends,
along with items
whose meaning is uncertain
after being separated
from their owner.
Although it will take
loving memories
of that life
to make such relics
truly come alive,
perhaps, a box or two,
is not so meager,
after all,
recognizing
that in the past,
the sole record
of one's existence
was often
one's name, alone.

ROSEBUDS

Gather rosebuds
while you can.

It will no longer
be a treat
after bending down
and getting back up
have become
an Olympic feat.

By then, you may find
a need to keep in mind
the purpose of your quest,
lest it be forgotten
by the time
the prize is at hand.

Despite the fact
that you have
a cataract,
take care
to avoid the thorns
that come your way.

And be sure
to hear the sound
of that bee,
especially,
if it is the one
you did not see.

You must not fret,
if the scent
that you get
appears somewhat faint
and quite hard
to locate.

In the end, it is wise
to accept your fate,
as it is already too late
if you can no longer
find some humor
in this tale.

VI

LOVE

AND

A SHORT HISTORY OF TENDING

Meanwhile our tending skills have been put to good use.

A CLIVIA OR TWO

Within two years of the armistice
Emma C. did the unthinkable.
She sold that certain lot of land
with the buildings thereon to Ida E.,
a woman with four of six sons
already born, creating a block
that multiple children would call home.
That Suburban Avenue off Main
would never again be the same.

As the years went by and life
receded from the porches,
few arrived at the heavy, old
oak and windowed front door
with its elaborate brass knob,
on their way to a second
and the built-in bench, upon which
plants were then quietly seated
as fewer guests needed to be greeted.

On that bench sat a clivia
in a dark brown ceramic pot
dating from an earlier era.
How that plant, a gift to Grandma,
ever managed to survive
in a house long shuttered after she died
remains something of a puzzle.
It appears the glass of water that Dad
threw on from time to time helped a tad.

Perhaps that even coincided
with the dormant time
the plant apparently required.
Having survived two generations,
it was now on its third owner.
After all that, it only seemed right
for the plant to have some company.
So, at a house sale another was bought
for less than one might have thought.

Thereafter, finding a proper home
for the new arrival,
with the right amount of food,
water, temperature and light,
proved to be a challenge,
as its long emerald green leaves
slowly, but determinedly,
turned yellow and fell off one by one,
until there were almost none.

Finally, a flower stalk
began to sprout, taking forever
to flower, and when it did,
that was when the surprise occurred.
There was not even one cluster
of the expected orange blooms.
In their stead, four pink ones appeared,
providing a way for all to see
its true identity.

That arrangement was the final proof.
The plant, in fact, was not a clivia.
Instead, it turned out to be
a giant amaryllis.
Hopefully, these cousins will in time
recognize their common bond and,
despite a difference in genus,
they will celebrate their family tie,
one that they should not deny.

ON HOLD

"Your call is very important to us."

That is why we have not provided adequate staffing for this line.

"A representative will be with you in just a moment."

Remember that your Mother warned you not to believe everything you were told.

"We appreciate your patience."

That is to say, you will need a lot of it.

"Your call will be answered in the order in which it was received."

Yet, if no calls are answered, this won't matter very much.

"Assistance is only a moment away."

Again, remember what your Mother told you.

"Please do not hang up and redial us. This will only further delay your call."

That is another way of saying that
nothing you do will help.

"You are caller number 2 in the queue."

Do not expect to become caller number
1 in a hurry. In any case, after that
you will become caller number 0 in
the queue and with no callers in the
queue, we will then disconnect.

Besides, this message is from another
line on which you are also on hold.
What would happen if both lines
answered at the same time?

You would have to put one of us on
hold. That would be unacceptable and
a waste of our time. Instead, we
recommend that you call back and, when
you again find yourself on hold, you
could put your time to good use and
write a poem.

"Please be assured that your call will
be answered as soon as possible."

By now, you know the drill. As an
alternative, why not try us on line.
There, it will take far less time for
you to become totally confused and
equally frustrated.

I WANTED TO SAY

The day will come
when the fun is done.
Then it will no longer be
all about you.
I wanted to say.

Contrary to what you think,
you are not always right
and, truth be told,
I am not always wrong.
I so wanted to say.

In this life
the only certainty,
other than the obvious one,
is uncertainty.
I thought about saying.

An affordable
insurance policy
against all perils
probably doesn't exist.
It occurred to me to say.

Few always win
and few always lose.
If you haven't tried both,
you haven't really lived.
I could have said.

Just because you want it
doesn't mean you get it.
But that is even more unlikely
if you don't even try.
I surely should have said.

Experience
will teach you
the error of your ways,
even if I can't.
I felt like saying.

You may not see
what I mean or hear me,
but don't tell me
I didn't warn you.
I really wanted to say.

THE WINDOW

There is
a special window
that provides
a different
point of view.

It opens
outside in
and permits
another train
of thought.

In the undergrowth
of daily life,
completing tasks
may become
a full time job.

The burden
of such obligations
will often
close off
other paths.

And a constant stream
of distractions
may leave little room
for contemplation
above the canopy.

But when one can pry
that window open,
a gentle breeze
may clear away
the clutter.

Once the lay
of the land
has been surveyed,
imagination
has room to sprout.

Creativity
may follow,
emerging
from the recesses
of the mind.

And the poems
waiting to be born
might then decide
to announce
their arrival.

THE SPIRIT OF SPRING

The spirit of spring
was due to appear
before the Ides
of March.

That is to say,
spring was on its way,
but its appearance
might be fleeting.

Spirit did not mean
the occurrence
would be a mistake
or aberration.

However, it did imply
that the day
would not begin
a trend.

Spirit promised
only a hint
or taste of what
there was to come.

Upon arrival, the day
announced a welcome shift
in season that would happen
at some future date.

What could be savored
in the meantime
was a brief moment
of perfection.

The sun was warm and
a sweet perfume wafted
in the breeze, without
a single bloom in sight.

An overwhelming
freshness in the air
seemed to stir the soul
of every living thing.

And that wondrous feeling
during a pandemic
offered added hope
that change was on the way.

THE OTHER

I believe that, growing up,
there is often another,
against whom one measures
oneself, only to sometimes
come up short.

In my case, I had to share
my name with an other
and my namesake
did not even spell
his name the right way.

It was a nuisance not knowing
who was being called and once
it got him into trouble,
something he did not
then deserve.

One day a bully forced me
to do his homework.
A teacher soon caught up
with him, suspicious
of his perfect score.

The other denied involvement
and the truth soon emerged.
I was admonished, but not punished,
as, even then, the power
of a bully was understood.

Before we went our separate ways,
the other was the first among us
to grow taller and lose the last
of his baby fat, something
the girls all seemed to notice.

Over the years, our paths crossed
only once, when he picked up
the phone of a business
I had called and gave his name,
as he had been instructed.

Decades later, I learned
that he had died, survived
by a loving family,
apparently having led
a life well lived.

In the end, differences
were not so important
and comparisons
no longer needed
to be made.

WITHOUT SQUIRRELS

Without squirrels,
there are peaches.

What led to this discovery,
as you will soon see,
began with a change
in the weather.

Despite the onset of cold,
the grass remained green,
something readily seen
in the absence of snow.

The slow start to winter
did little to hinder
outdoor dining among the wildlife,
though new rules led to confusion.

The apparent change in clime
gave the squirrels more time
to search for acorns, but that
led to other surprises.

It also delayed the start
of their annual siesta.
But, as it turned out,
that might not have been smart.

What became a matter of concern
was their failure to reappear
by the usual spring day
to collect their overtime pay.

By contrast, the bees stayed on schedule.
According to plan, they congregated
and then fully pollinated
the nearby peach tree.

Following that, the squirrels
would normally have climbed to its top
and, without receiving instructions,
would have denuded it in sections.

This year, they were nowhere to be found.
That seemed odd, since they never tired,
so, I first thought they conspired
to engage in some kind of work stoppage.

More likely, the role of nature
may have come into play,
with feral cats and birds of prey
adding peach thieves to their diet.

Their ranks may have been thinned out
by disease or infection
due to an absence of caution
when they went about their tasks.

At the same time, the rabbits
stopped eating the fallen peaches,
missing out on the treat
spread around at their feet.

In view of all this, it was wise
to remain close by, since the fruit
reached a marketable size
for the first time in years.

With such tangible proof in hand,
it is easy to understand
that without squirrels
there are peaches.

In addition, I can conceive,
and am inclined to believe,
that expressions are generally
born of observations.

Those who first described
failed attempts as fruitless
had no doubt already experienced
problems with squirrels.

SHOWN UP BY SHAKESPEARE

Shown up by Shakespeare, yet again.
When will the frustration ever end?

The man's been dead
for over four hundred years,
but what he wrote
still brings us to tears.

His oeuvre includes sonnets,
poems, plays and assorted verse.
Much of it is brilliant,
as well as quite diverse.

I spent the better part
of last week on a poem,
searching for some way
to express what I wished to say.

Despite trying so hard,
no one would mistake
what I produced
for the work of the Bard.

I hope that once I am
as old and cold as he
some of my words will be
remembered for their majesty.

Yet, I am afraid
when all is said and done,
the recognition I receive
will likely be none.

HISTORY

History is like porridge.
Each should be savored
and neither should be
prepared too dry.

If the portions are too large,
they may not be readily digested
and, if too small, their utility
could be questioned.

To encourage the consumption
of additional helpings,
a careful balance
must be achieved.

Noting what has not worked,
as well as what has succeeded,
can help with preparations
for the future.

Otherwise, it may be hard
to determine the ingredients
that will most likely lead
to repeated failure.

After all, failing to learn
from past mistakes in both
history and porridge is often
a recipe for disaster.

SMALL THINGS

Small things
loom large
these days
as worries
grow more
intense.

It is unclear
if youth
was ever
as carefree
as it was said
to be.

In any case,
that was long ago.
Experience and
the chemistry of age
have changed the way
life is perceived.

The day
may come
when memories fade
and cares
no longer
resonate.

Yet, more
must go astray
to reach that state
than is likely
to be
desired.

So, eliminating
all that worries me
may not be
as appealing
as it at first
might seem.

Instead,
selective
downsizing
may be all
that is
required.

A SHORT HISTORY OF TENDING

Tending began long ago,
given how helpless
our newborns are at birth.
While some were content
to hunt and gather,
others settled down
and began to tend gardens,
flocks and herds.

Today, the beds many tend
are more often filled
with flowers than with fruit.
And, the animals with whom
we now share our homes
are more likely to be pets
than to appear on the menu
as the main course.

Meanwhile, our tending skills
have been put to good use.
Freed from the toil of working
the soil and corralling livestock,
we have found other ways
to spend our time and can focus
our attention on a variety
of different chores.

We spend our days
cleaning, refilling,
recharging and repairing
the machines we have designed
to save us time and effort.
And, the more complex they become,
the more work it seems to take
to keep them running smoothly.

When not tending to them,
we manage to stay busy
searching for new ones,
as the machines we employ
often either predecease us
or become outmoded,
and, before we know it,
we need replacements.

While our tending has changed
over the years, it still takes up
much of the free time we thought
we had created, so those who tend
machines as a hobby or profession
are quite fortunate, indeed,
and the rest of us remain
frustrated by the effort.

SOMETHING TO SAY

To err is human.
So is wanting to speak.
Sometimes the two
even go hand in hand.

The need to verbalize
begins early, not only
to exercise those lungs,
but also, to make a point.

Normally, we desire
to be heard when speaking,
except when that
would be a mistake.

At such times, it would be well
if the need to speak
outweighed the desire
to be heard.

Then, even a cry
in the wilderness
might suffice to satisfy
what we seem to seek.

When communication
is a major goal,
the wish to be heard
will come to dominate.

Don't politicians and singers
expect others to listen,
except when they warm up
in the shower?

And, what actor, dancer,
musician or magician
prefers not to have
an audience?

Few artists and writers
want what they express
through their work to be
hidden from public view.

And, from the start,
children rarely wish
to be seen
and not heard.

After all,
don't they often
have something to say
until we ask about school?

LOVE 12

It takes
a bitter pill
to cure love
and, in fact,
one pill, alone,
may not suffice.
For that,
a steady diet
may be required.

For what has been
renounced,
rejected and
repudiated
may later be
reaffirmed,
reclaimed,
and again
relished.

What has been
rescinded,
reduced and
repressed
may be
resurrected
if it can be
renewed
and replenished.

And, just because
love has been
relegated to the past,
and remained
dormant for years
does not mean
it can not be
rediscovered
and reawakened.

Love may be
rebuffed
and then
redirected,
but when
it is re-examined,
the result could be
that it is
reimagined.

Yet, sometimes,
the best hope
for rekindling love
comes instead
from the introduction
of a new
love interest
and its response
in kind.

THE TIPPING POINT

There comes a time
when a tipping point
is reached,
due, in part,
to the backlog
of experience
we accumulate.
The vast knowledge
of possible outcomes
we acquire may become
a heavy burden
as well as a useful guide.
When competence and desire
have begun to wane,
we may find the weight
to be too great.
But once we understand
what is at play,
we may find the means
to chase the clouds away.

VII

LOVE

AND

THE END OF THE ISLAND

We move from conquest to conquest, exploring the world around us….

THE EVOLUTION OF CHANGE

Change has
an allure
and magic
all its own,
conjuring up
solutions
to our every woe,
but it also
may destroy
much
of what we know.
Perhaps, that is why
we come to fear
and abhor it so.

Once mastered,
change serves
as a weapon
for us to mold
the world we find
and upset
the status quo.
Yet, over time,
we come to see
why we should leave things
as they seem to be,
and the familiar
then becomes
our new best friend.

Once the next generation
has had the chance
to change the world
as it sees fit,
the world may become
an unfamiliar place,
inducing us
to seek change,
yet anew,
in order to modify
our point of view
and find
the comfort
that we crave.

In this task,
we must often proceed
without the certainty
we enjoyed
in our youth
and in the face
of conflicting
advice.
We are then left
with the wisdom
of age
and that may well
have
to suffice.

INSPECTED BY RUTH

The universe is
a mysterious place,
made up of complex
riddles quite often
beyond the understanding
of the human race.

It has its own rules,
but each time a puzzle
seems to get solved,
another arises
that may take decades
to be resolved.

Sometimes the issue
is closer to home
as with the label,
"Inspected by Ruth,"
I found on an old sweater
worn in inclement weather.

That label appeared
all of a sudden,
and try as I may,
I cannot say
why I did not see it
until that day.

Opposing schools of thought
soon made great haste
to begin explorations
of the facts of the case,
only to arrive
at different conclusions.

Each seemed to have merit,
but was hardly conclusive.
One argued that the label
had always been there,
but why it was not noticed
still remained elusive.

The other claimed the label
never belonged on the sweater,
but that is where it came to rest
one day when it fell off
some other item of clothing.
Yet, that seems chancy at best.

Much like matter's first appearance
in the emptiness of space,
something that is far more vital
to our continued survival,
the label's sudden arrival
can not be readily explained.

Perhaps Ruth has the answer,
if only we could find her.

GREAT ART

The answer
to a question
will often change
over time
and frequently
it just
depends.

Yet,
how
great art
is made
has remained
the same
for centuries.

To create
great art,
it takes
one artist
to create the art,
and, after that,
many to applaud.

THE END OF THE ISLAND

Close up,
it does not look
like much,
with its streaks
and smears of paint
on Masonite.

But, after stepping back
just a few feet,
a glorious vista
starts to appear.
With added light,
the painting begins to glow.

For her, it captures
endless summers
with extended family
gathered at the shore
and afternoon walks
to the end of the island.

For him, it does not evoke
a specific vista from the past,
but rather, the exhilaration
that we feel when we discover
new worlds that seem to stretch
as far as the eye can see.

How wonderful it is
to first encounter
what lies just on the other side,
around the corner, down the block,
through the woods, over the hill,
or deep in outer space.

Filled with anticipation,
we experience excitement
when we draw back the curtain
on the unknown
and reveal a landscape
with endless possibilities.

In those first few moments,
after conquering our fear,
we become the master
of all that we survey,
building the confidence
needed to take the next step.

We move from conquest to conquest,
exploring the world around us
and claiming each discovery
as a personal triumph,
as if no one
had ventured there before.

THE PENCIL

Sometimes I think
I am becoming obsolete
like that golden yellow
no. 2 soft pencil
I have just sharpened.

I wonder where it came from
and how such a relic
has remained pristine,
hardly showing any wear,
although produced so long ago.

What will the future bring?
Since children master
video games long before they learn
to write, or rather, print,
what needs will a pencil serve?

Perhaps, in a quiet moment,
when the computer is down
and there is no internet,
a pencil will prove useful
to jot down what we think.

Yet, there is never a guarantee
that others will understand
the words we have written,
whether or not obsolescence
was involved in their creation.

LOVE 13

With true love
you can not
just walk away,
try as you may.

Once bitten,
you will likely
remain
quite smitten.

Though true love
may be diminished,
it can rarely
be extinguished.

Even an innocent glance
will be taken as proof
that what is needed
is just one more chance.

Sometimes the search
for encouragement
will proceed in vain,
accompanied by pain.

In such a situation,
continued frustration
will be the result
if there is no "we"
and the song that is sung
does not become a duet.

NEARLY A DECADE LATER

Another year has come
and gone and there is
no doubt that we are
at least a year older.

The seventies were supposed
to be the new fifties,
but nearly half way in,
things seem somewhat touch and go.

Organs that had never
been heard from, now complain
that they shouldn't be asked
to do what they are told.

And while medicines can reduce
pain and make it seem
that little has changed,
it is not really so.

Though we greatly admire
what such remedies do,
there are sometimes effects
that we do not desire.

Fortunately, operations
are now routine that were
once experimental and
parts can be ordered on line.

Yet, what we often took
for granted in the days
when we felt immortal,
can rarely be equaled.

In the end, it is amazing
that we have been able
to retain so much
of the original design.

So, even if we are now
a bit fragile, the miracle
is that we have managed
to stay so well for so long.

THAT POEM

I would like
to write a poem
that will be read,
one that sings
so that music plays
each time it is recited,
one that can be understood
so that it speaks
to those who hear it,
one that is so clear
that its truth
can be recognized
without the use
of an interpreter,
both now
and in the future,
one that touches
a shared nerve,
revealing insight
into what is called
the human condition
and whose beauty
can be enjoyed
without a guide.
How does that sound
to you?

MY CLOSETS

What is in
my closets?
Nothing less
than the past,
present and future,
a timeline
of my travels,
along with the tastes
and various styles
I have embraced,
in addition to a lot
of this and that,
retained in case
I might someday need
a few of these and those,
which ones, precisely,
will be put to use,
I can not say,
since my future,
as well as theirs,
remains uncertain,
but I know full well
that as soon
as I thin out
my holdings,
what has been shed
will be sorely missed,
so, more is added
than is removed,

with the hope
that will help me face
what comes my way,
though it also creates
a lack of space
for the essential
acquisitions
that will surely follow,
requiring yet another
reorganization
of my storage vaults
to accommodate
my latest finds,
proving once again
that as the universe
continues to expand
at an ever
increasing rate,
so, too, can
and must
my closets.

WHEN IN DOUBT

When in doubt,
let it be Spring,
when so much
is new and fresh,
sweetness is
in the air
and little appears
worse for wear.

Summer has
its virtues, too,
as its days are long,
yet somehow
it always seems
shorter than required,
giving way to Fall
before that is desired.

When in doubt,
let it be Spring,
when hope is
pervasive,
things are surely
bound to succeed
and the possibilities
appear endless, indeed.

Fall may be
beautiful in parts
of the world,
with bright colors
and strong shadows,
but it can become barren,
cold and quite gray
all of a sudden.

When in doubt,
let it be Spring,
when there is
such joy, change
is welcome and,
with many openings,
the attention
is on that, not closings.

While Winter
has its charms,
there comes a time
when the cold is
no longer easy to bear
and it is beginnings
that are treasured
far more than endings.

So, when in doubt,
just let it be Spring!

REUNIONS

They were
quite young
a short time
ago,
or so it seemed,
although
more than half
a lifetime
has, in fact,
gone by.

In the early days,
they appeared
to be much the same,
with just a dash
of maturity added.
The wider world,
along with family
and a job or two,
can have that effect,
you know.

And, for a time,
while some things
did change,
here and there,
it was only
around the edges.
For the most part,
what you saw and heard
was what you remembered.

Slowly, however,
the now
and the then
began to diverge,
and in order
to connect the two
a leap of faith
and a bit of
reimagining
were required.

More and more
came to be
unfamiliar.
And, as I found
it difficult
to recognize them,
no doubt they, too,
must have wondered
what had become
of me.

EQUALITY

The desire for equality
comes early in life,
about at the time
sharing is required.

Once a first-born
is dethroned by one
or more siblings,
it begins in earnest.

For parents, this is
no simple matter,
as equal division
may not be possible or best.

The supply may be
limited and the needs
may be unequal.
Some need more, others less.

But consistently
favoring one over others
is clearly asking
for trouble.

It creates expectations
that rewards
will routinely follow
from demands.

That may lead
to disappointment,
as only a few will get
all they want.

The cost to others
of always satisfying
such demands
will be high.

Better to learn early
that you don't always get
what you want and that
you can survive even though
you sometimes have to share.

CANDLES

Candles vary
a lot,
one from another.
Some are
handcrafted,
while many more
appear to come
from the same mold.

There are those
that burn
brightly
for years,
while others
are snuffed out
long before
they are
fully consumed.

In some cases,
their wicks
are never
ignited and
one never learns
the extent
of their
glow.

They may remain
idle for years
and be viewed
as decorative
or be set aside
in anticipation
of a future
that never arrives.

Yet, until a candle
is either exhausted
or discarded,
there is always
the chance
that it can
light our way
or that of others.

THE PURPLE COW

At some time
early in my life
I was apparently fond
of a purple cow.

Being so well loved,
that cow was clearly
both handled and dropped
a number of times.

It has a smile
that is somewhat beguiling,
despite all the chips
that are there.

Because it is ceramic
in nature, it can not make
a single sound, but it must
have spoken volumes to me.

And I, for my part,
must have had a lot
to say for myself,
about what I do not know.

Alas, now it does not speak
to me the way it once did.
I hope it will find itself
in the hands of another.

Perhaps someone much younger
will pick up where I left off,
regard it as intriguing,
and get it to speak.

I would love to hear
some of that exchange
and be reminded of what
I may have heard.

As to my side
of the conversation,
my parents might have recalled
what I said. Just one more thing
I should have asked them about
while I had the chance.

ACKNOWLEDGMENTS

The publication of these poems would not have been possible without the encouragement, advice and expertise of many friends, family members and professionals.

My brother, Robert, was especially helpful. His intuitive sense of what needed further work proved to be invaluable. My sister-in-law, Nancy, niece, Holly, nephew, Scott, and their families, along with my cousins, Bonnie, Cathy, Jane, Jeff, Linda, and Nancy followed my progress most closely.

Friends and colleagues also graciously acted as sounding boards helping me to ensure that what I wrote resonated with others. In alphabetical order, those whom I called upon most frequently were: Jutta and Hans Bertram-Nothnagel, Robert H. Bull, Maria S. Campos, Linda L. Dennery, Jean Efron, Judith F. Hernstadt, Helen Hersh and Charles Sporn, Douglas P. Karp, Richard and Joanne Liddy, Randall and Carolyn McFarlane, Ahmed Mohamed, Fergal O'Neill, Clyde E. and Camille Rankin, Barbara Paul and Charles R. Robinson, Polly N. Rubin, Geoffrey C. Thomas, Patricia and Wayne Warnken, Ann T. Welles and family, Michael and Gerrie Wiles.

I have been inspired over many years by the love of language and dedication to sharing it exhibited by members of the poetry community. My original contact with the community was through Poets House and the poets, directors, and staff led by Lee Briccetti and Jane Preston associated with it.

I will long remember how welcoming and supportive Elizabeth Kray, Stanley Kunitz, Anne-Marie Levine, Myra Shapiro, Margo Viscusi and their family members were to me long before I ever considered writing a poem. I am also most grateful for the graciousness with which Elizabeth Coleman, Helen H. Houghton, Michael Salcman and others have greeted me and the opportunity they have provided for me to share my work.

In the process of preparing this book for publication, I relied greatly on my friends, Linda L. Dennery, Helen Hersh and Earl W. Zubkoff, whose guidance, technical skills, publishing experience and astute sense of design were of immense help throughout this project.

Finally, the enthusiastic support and professionalism of the team at Atmosphere Press made the publication of this book possible. For that, I am most grateful.

ABOUT ATMOSPHERE PRESS

Atmosphere Press is an independent, full-service publisher for excellent books in all genres and for all audiences. Learn more about what we do at atmospherepress.com.

We encourage you to check out some of Atmosphere's latest releases, which are available at Amazon.com and via order from your local bookstore:

Melody in Exile, by S.T. Grant

Covenant, by Kate Carter

Near Scattered Praise Lies Our Substantial Endeavor, by Ron Penoyer

Weightless, Woven Words, by Umar Siddiqui

Journeying: Flying, Family, Foraging, by Nicholas Ranson

Lexicon of the Body, by DM Wallace

Controlling Chaos, by Michael Estabrook

Almost a Memoir, by M.C. Rydel

Throwing the Bones, by Caitlin Jackson

Like Fire and Ice, by Eli

Sway, by Tricia Johnson

A Patient Hunger, by Skip Renker

Lies of an Indispensable Nation: Poems About the American Invasions of Iraq and Afghanistan, by Lilvia Soto

The Carcass Undressed, by Linda Eguiliz

ABOUT THE AUTHOR

Readers of this book will notice occasional legal or historical references, a foreign word or two, and an appreciation of art, science, and the creative process. This is hardly surprising given the author's legal career as a trusts and estates attorney, study of history, love of travel and passion for contemporary crafts and antiques. Undergraduate studies at Dartmouth College and graduate work in law and history at Yale University helped to nurture many of these interests. Writing these poems expanded the author's fascination with words through the discovery of their musical quality and their ability to convey nuance in describing human nature.